Healing Our Beginning

Sheila Fabricant Linn
Dennis Linn
Matthew Linn

Paulist Press
New York/Mahwah, N.J.

Cover and book design by Sharyn Banks
Cover and interior art by Francisco Miranda

Library of Congress Cataloging-in-Publication Data

Linn, Sheila Fabricant.
    Healing our beginning / Sheila Fabricant Linn, Dennis Linn, Matthew Linn.
        p. cm.
    ISBN 0-8091-4330-5 (alk. paper)
    1. Childbirth—Religious aspects—Catholic Church. 2. Psychic trauma—Religious aspects—Catholic Church. 3. Fetal behavior—Miscellanea. 4. Spiritual healing. I. Linn, Dennis. II. Linn, Matthew. III. Title.

    BX1795.C48L56 2005
    234'.131—dc22

                                                    2005009268

Published by Paulist Press
997 Macarthur Boulevard
Mahwah, New Jersey 07430

www.paulistpress.com

Printed and bound in the
United States of America

Contents

This book is lovingly dedicated to
Margaret Grant
and
John Matthew Linn
in gratitude for all they have taught us.

Chapter 1

Why Should We Try to Heal Hurts We Can't Even Remember?

Laura gave birth to a healthy baby, Anna, who was peaceful, happy and nursed well all day. However, around 10:00 each evening, Anna began to cry in an agitated, tense way that came in waves. She could not nurse, evidently because she could not coordinate her mouth. After a few days, Laura realized this was happening at the time the hospital staff team had given her Pitocin, a commonly used obstetrical drug that makes contractions stronger. Pitocin overrides the natural rhythm of contractions and substitutes huge and overwhelming waves of pressure.

The next evening at 10:00 when Anna began the waves of agitated crying, Laura made deep eye contact with her and empathically verbalized for her what she (Anna) might have been feeling as the waves of Pitocin hit her. Anna listened intently and then calmed down. After several evenings of this, Anna stopped her 10:00 p.m. crying spells.

We (Dennis and Sheila) experienced something similar when our son, John, was a baby. Often when he cried, the reason seemed obvious (e.g., he was hungry or wet). But when John seemed to be crying for "no reason at all," we believe he often was trying to tell us about his birth. As Laura did for Anna, we tried to empathically verbalize for John what he might be feeling. When we got it right, he would suddenly stop crying and look at us, as if to say, "How did you know?" People sometimes ask us when we will tell John that he is adopted. We respond by saying that he has always known this, and has been telling us what it was like ever since he came to us when he was eleven days old.

In our ministry of giving healing retreats all over the world, many people have reported to the three of us experiences of recalling their birth or life in the womb and the healing they have found when they could share these memories. Such experiences have convinced us that memories of life in the womb, even as far back as conception, arise commonly and spontaneously.

For example, Linda Mathison began to collect experiential evidence for early memory after her two-year-old son had shared what sounded to Linda like prenatal and birth memories. After Linda asked other parents if they had had similar conversations with their children, she received over a thousand accounts of what appear to be prenatal and birth memories in children under five years of age.

How was it possible for these children to remember as far back as conception? Not long ago, medical science taught that a child could not remember before the age of two because his or her central nervous system was too immature. Today, however, the research of famed neuroscientist Candace Pert indicates that cells throughout the body are capable of memory through the mechanism of neuropeptides (information molecules manufactured by nerve cells) and their receptors.

Pert and others go even further, and suggest an immaterial basis for memory. For example, Rupert Sheldrake's theory is that memory is not really in the brain. Rather, memory is in a field that surrounds us and our brains are like TV receivers that tune in to that field. Research on non-local communication, and on non-ordinary states of consciousness such as near-death experiences (in which people leave their brain and body and remember information they acquired while they were gone), seem to support the idea that memory is non-physical and spiritual in nature, and thus is not confined to the brain. This would explain how memory can go all the way back to conception, when the child has a fully conscious spirit but as yet no brain.

A Paradigm Shift

Such research has changed the way we think about early memory and early wounding. When Freud proposed that early childhood traumas can cause difficulty in adulthood, he initiated a major paradigm shift. More recently, the work of prenatal and perinatal researchers (such as Frank Lake, Graham

Farrant, David Chamberlain and Thomas Verny) represents another major paradigm shift, in which the origin of wounding begins not in childhood but rather at the first moment of our existence. Frank Lake goes so far as to say that the origin of psychoses, the most serious mental illnesses, is in the womb.

The Western cultural assumption that human beings grow in consciousness as they mature is only half the truth. The opposite is also true: At conception we come here with a fully formed spirit, straight from the heart of God. We come fully conscious, and we have not yet numbed ourselves out in order to defend ourselves against hurts. Although we are not yet cognitively developed, we are fully aware energetically and spiritually. We know the "feel" and the intention of everyone and everything around us. One reason prenatal and perinatal trauma can be so wounding is that we feel so alone with this knowing. We are as exquisitely sensitive, if not more so, than at any other time in life...in a culture that for the most part believes a baby in the womb is an unconscious blob.

Because we are so exquisitely conscious at the beginning, whatever happens to us then imprints upon us. Thus, the earliest hurts we experience are absorbed and stored in our cells and form a kind of template or remembered tone to which we continue to "vibrate sympathetically," as R. D. Laing puts it. Later hurts then become far more crippling than they otherwise might be. So, for example, a child who was not invited to her classmate's birthday party, or a woman whose husband left her, would be more devastated by this rejection if her own parents had not wanted to conceive her or had tried to abort her. Similarly, a child who was sent to preschool before he was ready, or a man whose home was broken into as an adult, would be more devastated by this violation of his sense of security if he was pulled from the womb by cesarean section or forceps.

We have seen this in our own lives. For example, I (Dennis) have tended to worry more about being late than I might otherwise because my birth took so long (i.e., I was so late) that I almost died. I (Sheila) have tended to doubt myself and assume I am wrong because my mother's pregnancy with me was regarded as a mistake by her family. I (Matt) struggle with a pessimistic tendency to believe things will only get worse, in part because I was conceived right after Pearl Harbor was attacked. My attitude toward life mirrors the dire headlines my parents were reading as my worried mother carried me in her womb. As these early wounds are healed, we each "vibrate sympathetically" less and less to their remembered tone.

How Can We Experience Our Parents' World While We Are in the Womb?

Research on early memory may help us understand how it is possible for us to remember prenatal events, but how do we become aware of those events in the first place? How could Sheila have known that her mother's family did not want her to be born? How could Matt have experienced his parents' fear while he was in the womb, to the extent that later he continually recapitulated fears related to World War II in his everyday life? At one level, Matt could have experienced his parents' world through his biological connection to his mother. Every emotion a pregnant woman feels produces chemical changes in her blood, which are then shared with her child as these emotions cross the placenta and enter the child's body through the umbilical cord. Just how quickly mother and child can share feelings is demonstrated by an experiment in which pregnant women were told their babies weren't moving. Each woman became alarmed that something might be wrong with her baby. Within seconds the baby, observed through ultrasound, was kicking—apparently in response to its mother's fear.

At a more subtle and mysterious level, babies have a spiritual connection to their parents and to their parents' world. Perhaps you can understand this by recalling a time when you have thought of a friend who was far away, and at that very moment you received a phone call from that person. Or you may have experienced entering a room and feeling uneasy, only to learn that a terrible argument has just taken place there. Clinical researchers have observed that babies, too, have intuitive radar that allows them to pick up feelings and subtle changes in their environment.

Beginning at the Beginning

Unfortunately, the environment in which many babies develop, even in the womb of a healthy mother, often includes trauma. Unresolved prenatal and perinatal trauma can have devastating long-term effects, not only on the individual but also on society. Several years ago, the State of California funded the first scientific study of the roots of violence and crime. The study concluded that a significant factor in the increase of violence in our culture is the separation of mother and infant at birth.

Why is the separation of mother and infant at birth predictive of violence? Erik Erikson identified the task of the first stage of life, infancy, as the formation of basic trust. If basic trust is not achieved, all later stages of development into a moral, loving and responsible adult are compromised. The "stuff" of trust in infancy is bonding, meaning a mutual process of attachment in which the adult experiences commitment to the baby and the baby experiences a secure sense of belonging to the adult. When mother and child are separated at birth—the moment when the child is most ready to begin the bonding process outside the womb—the child's capacity to trust is deeply wounded.

In our culture, other assaults on trust often follow. They include things we regard as "normal," such as circumcision, invasive medical procedures, insufficient breast-feeding, requiring infants to sleep alone in cribs, and putting babies in daycare after a standard six-week maternity leave. In addition, the language of babies—their crying—is often suppressed. Babies communicate their feelings through crying and for healthy bonding to occur, these feelings need to be empathically received.

Moreover, disruption in bonding can begin long before the separation of mother and child at birth. It can begin as early as conception through such things as ambivalence about the pregnancy, conflict or anger between the parents, substance abuse and sexuality that involves power, force or violence. All of these contribute to the current epidemic of violence among our adolescents and adults. In addition to violence, we also see symptoms of disrupted bonding in the pervasive cynicism, materialism (attachment to things rather than to persons) and emphasis upon self-interest throughout our society. Well-bonded human beings who have developed basic trust do not behave in these ways.

In an effort to address these problems, many concerned people in the United States have promoted Head Start (a program of intellectual and social enrichment for deprived pre-school-age children). More recently, Early Head Start was designed to focus on even younger children, from ages zero to three. In Venezuela, from 1979 to 1984, the government promoted Project Family. Like Early Head Start, it was designed to stimulate the full development of children from poor families, beginning at birth. However, in comparison with their peers, the gains made by the children in Project Family were only temporary.

The director of Project Family, Dr. Beatriz Manrique, realized that in order to have a lasting impact she needed to begin earlier, in the womb. She designed an enrichment program called "Hello Baby" that began during the fifth month of gestation and continued until age six. A follow-up study of these children showed that they made lasting physical, emotional, intellectual and social gains. Hello Baby demonstrates that programs like Head Start—even Early Head Start—are too late. If we really want to help our children, ourselves and our culture, we have to begin at the beginning.

Chapter 2

Healing of Prenatal and Perinatal Trauma Is for Everyone

We have seen many people healed when in prayer they spontaneously regressed to birth, the womb or even conception. They have shared with us how Jesus, Mary, or another trusted figure entered the scene and helped them. I (Sheila) experienced this during a guided meditation focused on my birth. I felt terror and grief at the realization that I would have to leave the womb. Although my birth was very difficult physically, that was not my primary concern. Rather, I was aware that I was being born to parents who would not be able to *see* me—really see me as myself. I could remember the heart of God behind me. I knew I had been seen there and I felt great despair at losing that.

I asked for help and an image came to me of a small, ancient house in the old city of Jerusalem, overlooking a val-

ley to the west. In the doorway was a rocking chair. Although Jesus did not live in Jerusalem as far as we know, I imagined him there, at home with his family. One or another of them held me and rocked me in the chair. I had the sense that I was rocking across eternity.

As I rocked in the chair, I realized that the same eternal depth of being lived within me. The scene that surrounded me in the doorway of Jesus' home was a mirror of my spirit. I felt even more deeply my longing to be seen at birth, in all my depth and as clearly as the one who held me in the chair could see me. Then I realized I came here knowing that eventually I would meet Denny and he would see me. With that, I felt willing to be born. It occurred to me that Jesus' family would go with me as I left the womb and I could simply rock my way out. So, that's what I imagined myself doing. It was easy and joyful.

Since then, I have felt a new conviction that the loving light from which I came will never leave me, and that I am *seen* as I live out my life here. Moreover, it's all right to *be* seen. Although I often speak to large groups, and am usually quite comfortable, before this process I felt extreme shyness and self-consciousness in any group in which I was not the speaker. Now I am comfortable being seen by others, even when I do not have the protection of the special role of speaker.

I (Dennis) grew up with a fear of women and of sexuality. I never dated in high school, and for the next twenty-seven years I lived in a celibate religious community. After I learned about healing prayer, I asked myself what I wanted from Jesus' life. I realized that I wanted to go to Bethlehem and be held and breast-fed by Mary, as Jesus was. I did this every day for two or three months until the desire for it was gone. During the next several months, I noticed that my fear of women gradually disappeared. I formed healthy friendships with women and experienced a new sense of wholeness in my sexual identity. It is a miracle to me that now I am happily married to Sheila.

I could have spent years trying to figure out the origin of my fear of women. Often such introspection, perhaps with the help of a therapist and/or a spiritual companion, would be very valuable for personal growth. However, sometimes healing comes simply by asking for it. In this case, I asked Jesus for what I most wanted from his life, to be held by his mother. What I most wanted was what I most needed for healing, without having to figure it out in my head. Perhaps entering a scene from Jesus' life was so healing for me because biblical imagery is exquisitely and mysteriously designed to evoke the depths of our own inner life. The archetypal symbols of the Bible—rich as they are in prenatal and perinatal themes such as journeys, discoveries and homes—can activate our own wounds that are ready for healing, including those we were unaware of. We say "are ready for healing" because we trust that in an environment of love (rather than one of insensitive probing), generally only those traumas that are ready for healing will emerge into consciousness.

Our experience with healing prayer is confirmed by studies of the use of religious imagery. For example, in a study by psychologist L. R. Propst of depressed patients who scored high on measures of religiosity, some received therapy that encouraged religious imagery and others received the same therapy but without the use of religious imagery. Only fourteen percent of the patients in the first group remained depressed, compared to sixty percent of the patients in the second group, whose therapy did not include religious imagery.

Because religious imagery is so powerful and has been so healing of our own early trauma, we imagine our son John in Mary's womb. We recall the many times we have visited the Shrine of Our Lady of Guadalupe in Mexico City. Perhaps one reason so much healing has happened there is that Our Lady of Guadalupe wears a sash indicating that she is pregnant. Maybe the Mexican people and pilgrims from all over the world love her so much and keep returning to visit her because they have found a way to heal prenatal and perinatal trauma by relating to her. Thus we expect that bringing John to Mary's womb is healing him, especially as he sleeps, just as her breast-feeding healed Dennis and just as her presence at the Shrine of Our Lady of Guadalupe has healed so many pilgrims.

While the Mexican culture focuses on Our Lady of Guadalupe, in our culture many of our Christmas traditions are ways of healing our prenatal and perinatal trauma by imaginatively participating in Jesus' conception, gestation and birth. The crib scene, introduced by St. Francis of Assisi, is an especially popular way of preparing for Christmas. Francis took a donkey and an ox into a cave in the forest. Then he used wood and straw to build a manger, where he placed a carved wooden figure of the baby Jesus. Local villagers played the parts of Joseph, Mary and the shepherds. Hundreds of people came to see the crib scene and the night sky was lit up by their torches.

A knight who was present, John of Greccio, claimed that instead of a wooden figure he saw a beautiful child asleep in the manger crib, and that St. Francis took him in his arms and the child woke up. Our guess is that John of Greccio's own inner child realized his beauty and woke up. We don't know that, but we do know the people kept the hay from the crib as a reminder of what they experienced that night. The hay was said to heal their illnesses as well as cure their animals.

As children, all during Advent, after Sunday Mass, our (Dennis and Matt's) family would stand in line waiting our turn to carefully place straw in the church manger. The manger was empty (the child Jesus would be placed there on Christmas eve). In this way the entire church congregation participated in Jesus' gestation and birth. The crib scene has become a symbol for the whole Christian world of participation in Jesus' birth, rather like a collective projective technique.

The Italian and French painters did something similar. They painted the nativity scenes full of people who looked much like their own families, or the royal family that sponsored their painting. Perhaps they, too, were identifying with the life of Jesus in order to open their unconscious to receive healing from the crib scene. And from our point of view, this isn't just a projective technique—although it is that—but a way of actually accessing the healing love of God and letting it touch and heal our prenatal and perinatal wounds.

Healing Prenatal and Perinatal Trauma in the Gospels

When Francis of Assisi or the French and Italian painters imaginatively reconstruct scenes from Jesus' prenatal and perinatal life in ways that most fit their needs for healing, they are imitating the gospels. The account of Jesus' birth occurs in the Gospels of Matthew and Luke, and his birthplace is referred to in the Gospels of John and Mark, as well as elsewhere in the New Testament. Because the audiences of the gospel writers were as different from one another as the local villagers of Assisi were from the royal audiences of the French and Italian painters, the birth stories of each writer are very different. The events before, during and after Jesus' birth are reported so differently that it seems to many prominent scholars (such as Raymond Brown and John Meier) that no one person could do them all. For example:

- How could Jesus be born in both Bethlehem, as the Infancy Narratives in Luke and Matthew suggest, and at the same time be born in Nazareth as the entire rest of the New Testament assumes, including the Gospels of John (1:45, 7:41–42) and Mark (6:1–4)?

- How could Jesus be born in Joseph's home in Bethlehem, as Matthew suggests, and at the same time be

born in an abandoned stable far away from home as
Luke suggests?

- In Matthew's Gospel, the celebration of Jesus' birth is
cut short by the narrow escape of Jesus into Egypt in
order to avoid King Herod's slaughter of Jewish
babies. In Luke's Gospel, the celebration of Jesus'
birth continues. There is no King Herod, no slaughter of Jewish babies, no flight into Egypt. Instead,
Jesus returns home to Nazareth after his birth.

These discrepancies have led many scholars to conclude
that the gospel writers were not writing biographical history,
but rather symbolic history based upon images from the Old
Testament, in order to affirm that Jesus is Savior. We wonder
if they were also, perhaps unconsciously, trying to heal their
own prenatal and perinatal hurts and those of their readers.
Perhaps they told the story differently because their audiences were different and they were creating a safe and familiar environment in which hurts could be healed.

I (Sheila) did exactly the same thing with that scene of
the rocking chair in the ancient house in Jerusalem that I
mentioned at the beginning of this chapter. I imagine this as
Jesus' home, even though most scholars would probably
agree that Jesus was born and lived in Nazareth. However,
Jerusalem is extremely significant for *me*. Each time I've been
there I have felt especially close to my Jewish ancestors.
Thus, I am integrating a symbol of strength and comfort in
my own life (Jerusalem) with my experience of Jesus and his
family as sources of love. I'm imaginatively creating a safe

place, a "holding environment," an inner "eternal city" in which I can receive healing.

Healing and the Imagination

Some of the healing processes we will suggest in this book are based upon Christmas and other Christian feasts. All the healing processes are simple, using something available to everyone: our imagination. Events that we imagine can cause the same physiological changes as "real" events, and can have a similarly powerful effect upon our feelings and attitudes. For example, Dr. Antonio Madrid reports thirty cases of children whom he treated for asthma and whose bonding with their mothers had been disrupted at birth. Although Dr. Madrid used several methods of treatment, the major shift occurred when he encouraged the mothers to imagine the kind of loving birth they wished they and their child had shared. The result was that the children's asthma diminished or ceased entirely. This example illustrates the power of the imagination to heal not only asthma, but also underlying hurts such as disrupted bonding. We and those we care for can be healed when we bring love into our hurtful memories, no matter how deep or how early the trauma.

The Spiritual Exercises

When we use our imagination to heal early trauma (as in Dennis and Sheila's stories), we are doing what St. Ignatius recommends in the *Spiritual Exercises*, a retreat manual that is used as the basis for many retreats in the Catholic tradition. One common aspect of these spiritual exercises is to imagine oneself participating with Jesus in the events of his life as recorded in the gospels. The retreatant is encouraged to enter a given scene, identify with Jesus, and take in from Jesus whatever he or she needs for healing.

Although we doubt St. Ignatius ever heard the words "projective technique," he seems to have intuitively understood the need to imaginatively integrate one's own experience with Jesus' birth in a way that could bring healing. Even though Ignatius visited Jesus' birthplace and remembered it in detail, he encouraged retreatants to create their own pictures of the place where Jesus was born. For example, he writes that one should "observe the place or cave where Christ is born; whether big or little; whether high or low; and how it is arranged." Ignatius's words seem to us a medieval form of healing processes through which we can re-experience the womb and birth tunnel from which we came, "whether big or little, high or low," and whether or not its arrangement includes many obstacles.

Healing Process for Oneself

1. Light a candle and read the story of Jesus' birth in Luke 2:1–18.

2. Close your eyes and breathe deeply. If you wish, sing *Silent Night* softly to yourself and breathe in the peace of that night. You may wish to put your

hand on any part of your body where you think you may carry birth trauma.

3. Imagine "the place or cave where Christ is born; whether big or little; whether high or low; and how it is arranged." Now become the baby in the crib. Scrunch up your shoulders or your hands or your toes to help you feel smaller, like a baby. Use all your senses to enter the scene. Feel the straw between your toes and the cold night air in your nostrils. Let a shiver go up and down your spine. Hear the sounds of the animals, and smell their bodies near you in the stable. See the faces of Mary and Joseph leaning over you, and the starry night behind them.

4. Become aware of whatever it is you most need. Perhaps you are cold or wet or hungry. Maybe something has frightened you. You may be exhausted from struggling to be born. Perhaps you feel alone. Whatever you are feeling, imagine that you begin to cry. You may want to let the muscles of your face contort as they do when you cry.

5. Feel two hands reaching down to scoop you up and hold you. Are they the rough but loving hands of Joseph, the carpenter? Are they the smaller and gentler hands of Mary? Are they the hands of someone else?

6. For the next few minutes, let whoever is holding you love you and care for you in whatever way you most

need. Perhaps you need to be breast-fed, or held close and reassured, or stroked where your body was hurt in being born. Perhaps you need to hear that you are wanted and welcome. Let the one who is holding you delight in you in whatever way you need the most.

7. You may wish to end by once more singing *Silent Night* softly to yourself, breathing in the peace of that night.

Note: This book includes several healing processes, such as the one above. Neither these processes nor this book as a whole are intended as a substitute for professional treatment. If you have problems that require such treatment, we encourage you to seek help from trained medical and/or psychological professionals.

Chapter 3

The Journey of Conception

Several times recently, a friend (face full of wonder) has told us a version of the following story:

> A couple had a little girl and a newborn son. The girl kept asking to be alone with the baby. Her parents were afraid to allow it because they thought perhaps she was jealous of her new brother and would harm him. Finally they agreed to the child's request, but they listened in through the intercom in the newborn's room. The girl entered the room and at first all was quiet. Then the parents heard their daughter say to the baby, "Tell me about heaven. I'm beginning to forget."

Why does this story touch people so deeply, and why is it so widespread? Perhaps it is because the story reminds us of something we all knew. The psychiatrist Joan Fitzherbert writes that until around the age of two, children are in intimate contact with the mind of God. Their consciousness is only partially here—the rest is with the One from whom they came.

If the contrast between the One we came from and this world seems too great, we may deeply regret leaving the heart of God in order to enter the womb. For example, I (Dennis) was born into a family with a vengeful, punitive image of God. I did not want to be born because I was trying to return to the unconditionally loving God I had known. The womb seemed dark in comparison. Even my birth position seems to symbolize this: I was a breech birth (born feet first), perhaps because I was desperately reaching back for the light from which I came. In later life, this desperation led me to religious addiction, the multiplying of religious practices.

Are Babies Trying to Help Us Remember Our True Home?

Our (Dennis and Sheila's) first words to John were, "We will do all we can to help you remember where you came from." We suspect he is saying back to us, "I'm going to do all *I* can to help *you* remember where I came from."

For example, John's first spoken word to us (after "Mama") was, "light." Since early infancy, John's favorite places in the house were lamps and light switches, which he learned to operate when he was four months old. His favorite toy was a flashlight. Why was John so fascinated by light? And why, when he was most upset, was it light that comforted him (besides our arms and nursing at Sheila's breast)?[1] A friend who teaches pediatrics told us that fascination with light is very common among babies.

Could it be that light reminds babies of their original home in the heart of God? Light is a universal symbol of God and of heaven. For example, although they vary in other ways, the one detail that the gospel accounts of Jesus' birth have in common is that Jesus brought the light into darkness (Matt 2:2, Luke 2:8–9, John 1:5). We traditionally celebrate Christmas on December 25th, which ancient people in the northern hemisphere believed was the winter solstice. Thus, while people of other religions prayed for the return of the sun on the darkest night of the year, Christians transformed this custom into praying for the coming of Jesus, the Light of the World. This Christian theme of light is evident today in our use of lights to decorate homes, Christmas trees, Advent wreaths, and so on.

Light comes with us into this world. At its best, conception is a joyful union of egg and sperm in a biochemical explosion of light. All three participants (mother, father and child) are saying a wholehearted "Yes!"

We Remember Conception

We carry the memory of our conception, joyful or not. The psychiatrist Dr. Graham Farrant was a pioneer in the fields of cellular research and of healing prenatal and perinatal trauma. In 1979, he regressed in his imagination back to his own conception. In this experience, which was videotaped, two elements contradicted medical knowledge of conception at that time. First, Graham experienced the egg opening two "arms" to embrace a chosen sperm. Secondly, he experienced the fertilized egg hesitating in the fallopian tube, as if uncertain whether or not to go on.

Four years later, in 1983, the Karolinska Institute released the film "Miracle of Life," that showed the actual process of conception. Graham played this film side by side with the videotape of his 1979 regression. His own spontaneous movements during regression mirrored exactly what actually takes place during conception and what is now accepted medically. For example, contrary to the common perception that the sperm always aggressively penetrates the egg, we now know that the egg can actively participate in choosing and welcoming a particular sperm into itself. Similarly, we now know that the fertilized egg can hesitate on its journey down the fallopian tube.

Our experience of our conception is profoundly colored by the relationship between our parents. Thus violence, shame-based sexuality or drug abuse between the parents infuses the child's experience of conception with violence, shame or the distorted awareness caused by drugs. (Moreover, the use of cigarettes, alcohol or other drugs prior to conception by either parent can harm the sperm or the egg.) If a baby is conceived accidentally or is unwanted, the baby may feel as if he or she *is* a mistake. Conversely, if a child is conceived by parents who love and respect one another and who want that child, the child has a foundation for self-respect and the ability to give and receive love.

Healing Process for Oneself

The basis for a healthy life is to be at peace with God as the one who created us and with our own earthly existence.

1. Light a candle and read Luke 1:26–38, the Annunciation story in which the angel Gabriel proclaims to Mary that she will conceive a special child. Count backwards from your birth date to the probable date of your conception. Trust that there is a good reason for whatever date comes to you.

2. Now imagine yourself going all the way back to the beginning of your existence in the heart of God. Imagine God asking if you would be willing to come into this world.

3. Ask yourself, "Do I want to come?" and listen within your whole being for the answer.

4. If your answer is "Yes," imagine yourself coming into this world, enfolded in the loving light of God. Then ask yourself, "What would help me enter even more fully into life?" Imagine yourself receiving what you need as you breathe in God's creative and loving light.

5. If your answer is "No," ask yourself, "What would help me become willing to come here?" Perhaps you will think of a special person whose love would help you, a safe place in nature, an activity that gives

your life meaning, and so on. Whatever your answer, imagine yourself receiving what you need as you breathe in God's creative and loving light.

6. If you wish to continue, ask yourself what it was like to be conceived in the body of your mother. What was it like for your spirit to merge with matter? With your father's sperm? With your mother's egg? With the relationship between your parents? What did you most need?

7. If you wish, let your mother's body become the body of Mary. Imagine Mary resting her hands upon the place in her body where you are being conceived. Imagine Joseph standing protectively by her, with his hands over hers. Breathe in from Mary and Joseph (or your parents, or the most loving woman and man you know) whatever you most needed at the moment of your conception.

Healing Actions for Oneself

1. Swing on a swing. (Remember Sheila's rocking chair?) As you go backward, imagine that you are reaching back for your home in the heart of God. As you go forward, bring that home with you into this world.

2. Find a picture of your mother and put it in your pocket. Go for a long walk, imagining that you are your mother's egg, waiting for the sperm that will

become you. Notice what feelings and images come to
you as you walk. Whatever comes, breathe the healing love of God into yourself and into your mother.

3. Find a picture of your father and repeat the same
   process, imagining that you are your father's sperm,
   on its way to meet your mother's egg.

Healing Process for Unborn Children

Parents can pray this for a baby in the womb, or for an
older child.

1. Light a candle and read Luke 1:26–38.

2. Close your eyes and breathe deeply. One or both
   parents place their hands on the woman's body
   where the child was conceived. Count backward to
   the probable date of conception. Trust there is a
   good reason for whatever date comes to you.

3. Imagine your child being conceived in this body.
   What was it like for your child to be a spirit merg-
   ing with matter? To be merged with its father's
   sperm? To be merged with its mother's egg? To be
   merged with the relationship between its parents?
   What did your child most need?

4. Now breathe in from Mary and Joseph (or the most
   loving woman and man you know) whatever you
   imagine your child most needed at the moment of his
   or her conception. Breathe that out into your child.

Chapter 4

Early Pregnancy

A normal pregnancy is approximately thirty-eight to forty-two weeks long. During the first three months, physical development is especially critical. In fact, by the end of the first trimester all of the body's parts are developed, even though they must still mature. Trauma or stress interrupts the process of physical development and leaves long-term predispositions to illness, especially in those parts of the body that are in a critical period of development when the trauma takes place. For example, the human heart begins beating three weeks after conception, around the time of discovery. If the parents and extended family rejoice in the pregnancy, the baby's entire system knows it and the developing heart is likely to be strong. However, if the pregnancy is unwanted, this rejection is passed on to the baby. The baby's cardiac system, which is in a critical period of development, will be most affected.

For example, Dr. Graham Farrant, mentioned earlier, was born with a disease that damaged the ventricle wall of his heart. During a healing process in which he imagined himself back in the prenatal period, he experienced his mother trying to abort him by alternating hot and cold baths. He sensed this happened at exactly the most critical time for the development of the ventricle wall. He confronted his mother, who was astonished because she had never told anyone about the abortion attempt. She acknowledged that Graham's experience was correct. As the hurt of his mother's abortion attempt was healed, medically verified changes in Graham's heart occurred to the extent that he lived twenty years longer than medical experts expected.

While emotional factors affect the formation of physical systems, as in the case of Graham Farrant's heart, physical factors also affect emotional development. An example is the effect of smoking, drugs and alcohol during the earliest weeks of pregnancy, as described by Karr-Morse and Wiley:

> It appears that there is a period of great vulnerability to many types of drugs and to alcohol during the embryonic period, which is defined as the first eight weeks of pregnancy....Unfortunately, this is the time when many women are unaware that they are pregnant....Many experts believe that fetal alcohol exposure, particularly because it may occur undetected and go untreated, may well be the single largest factor setting up physical and neurological conditions that predispose American babies to aggressive and violent behavior.[1]

Toxic substances such as alcohol can damage the nervous system and can even alter genes, that are affected by the chemical and hormonal environment during gestation. Nicotine, which a former U.S. Surgeon General describes as "probably the single most important modifiable cause of poor pregnancy outcome," can cause brain cell damage. Thus, the baby's physical development is affected in such a way that healthy emotional growth may be disrupted.

Implantation

A critical event for both physical and emotional development during early pregnancy is implantation, when the baby implants into the uterine wall. Psychologically, a positive implantation experience affirms our ability to find and make for ourselves and others a home, where we put down roots and belong. If implantation is difficult for physiological reasons (such as fibroids, cysts, hardened tissue, etc.) and/or because of conscious or unconscious negative attitudes and feelings in the parents about conceiving a child, it may be difficult later in life to feel at home.

Discovery

Another critical event that shapes our sense of being at home is discovery, the moment (usually between three and six weeks after conception) when the mother first discovers she is carrying a child. Ideally, this is a moment of celebration in which the mother joyfully shares the good news with the father, family and friends. If joy and celebration are the prevailing attitudes of the parents when a child is discovered, for the rest of his life that child is likely to feel wanted and welcome in this world. He will feel confident of having a right to exist, take up space, be seen and make an impact on the world.

However, if the parents are not happy about the pregnancy, their child may have difficulty feeling wanted and welcome, and may struggle with issues ranging from shyness and insecurity to profound and crippling shame over her very existence. As an adult, she may find it hard to accept compliments and attention, and may often feel like hiding—or, on the other hand, seek compliments and attention throughout life, without knowing why.

I (Sheila) had what might be called "discovery trauma." My mother, who was emotionally disturbed, came from a very nice and well-respected family. They felt embarrassed by her and did not want her to have children. When they discovered that she was pregnant with me, their attitude was, "This baby will probably be disturbed like her mother and should not be born." Within the womb, I absorbed their attitude such that it became a template for my life. Until this was healed, I felt as if everyone was staring at me, pointing a finger and silently saying I should not exist.

Despite my family's attitude, I was allowed to live. However, discovery sometimes results in a decision to abort the baby. This is the most traumatic experience a child can have and profoundly disrupts bonding between mother and child. An attempted abortion can result in lifelong, pervasive feelings of shame, fear of annihilation, rage and self-destructive impulses.

For example, Dr. Andrew Feldmar had some patients who had attempted suicide five or more times, at the same time each year. The dates seemed meaningless until Dr. Feldmar realized that these patients were attempting suicide at a time that would be the anniversary of their second or third month in the womb. When he investigated their histories, Dr. Feldmar discovered that the dates of the suicide attempts were the dates when each one's mother had attempted an abortion. Even the method was similar. One patient, whose mother had tried to abort him with a darning needle, tried suicide with a razor blade. Another, whose mother had used chemicals, tried suicide with a drug overdose. When Dr. Feldmar's patients realized that their suicidal ideas were really memories of their mother's attempt to kill them, they no longer felt compelled to commit suicide.

We Need a Community to Delight in Us

We need to be joyfully welcomed not only at critical moments like discovery and implantation, but throughout life. For example, because our John had suffered separation from his birth mother, we (Dennis and Sheila) knew he needed an intense experience of welcome, not only from us but from a large community of family and friends. We sent a birth announcement to five hundred people, many of whom traveled to our home to attend John's baptism.

We believe the core of baptism is delight in and welcome of a new member of the community. Thus we asked each of our guests to bless John, one by one, with whatever most delighted them about him. For example, a person who noticed John's unusual focused attention blessed him with the gift of being present to others. Another person, knowing all John went through to be born, blessed him with the gift of overcoming obstacles.

Our guests were doing for John what empowered Jesus at his own baptism. When Jesus was baptized, he heard the words, "You are my beloved son in whom I am delighted" (Mark 1:11). Like Jesus, and our son, in order to know that we belong in this world, we all need to experience that others delight in our coming. Perhaps it is no accident that the person Jesus chose to baptize him was John the Baptist, his cousin. The basis of Jesus' and John the Baptist's relationship was delight, beginning thirty years before when they were both in the womb and John leapt for joy at Jesus' coming (Luke 1:44).

Healing Process for Oneself

This prayer is based upon the Visitation, when Elizabeth and her unborn child, John the Baptist, delight in Jesus. The Visitation celebrates the conscious life of the child in the womb, as the two babies (Jesus and John the Baptist) communicate with each other and become lifetime friends.

Because you are praying for a time when you were in an enclosed and darkened place, you may wish to do this prayer in a closet or some other small dark space. Notice which space feels exactly the right size for this stage of your development.

1. Light a candle and read Luke 1:39–56, the story of Mary's visit to Elizabeth.

2. Close your eyes and breathe deeply. Place your hand on your heart.

3. Imagine you are being carried in your mother's womb, under her heart. If your mother's womb was not a welcoming place, imagine you are carried in the womb of Mary or of the most loving woman you know. Feel the warm fluid around you. Hear the heartbeat above you and muffled sounds from the outer world.

4. Ask yourself whose delight in your coming would matter most to you. Invite those people to surround you as a baby in the womb. Perhaps you will also want to invite Mary's cousin (Elizabeth) and the baby in Elizabeth's womb (John the Baptist) to be present. Hear Elizabeth cry out to the woman who carries you, "The moment your greeting sounded in my ears, the baby leapt in my womb for joy." Let all the others whom you have invited express their joy over you and join Elizabeth and John the Baptist in blessing you.

5. Breathe in the love and welcome that surround you. Imagine it filling the moment when you actually were discovered. Let that love and welcome spread out through the entire first trimester, touching any moments that may have been difficult. Breathe love

into your body to heal the effects of alcohol, cigarettes, drugs, pollutants or other toxic substances your mother may have ingested.

Healing Actions for Oneself

1. Go to the place where you feel most at home. Ask yourself how you would like to change or add to this place, even in some very small way, so that you would feel even more at home. Do whatever comes to you.

2. Ask a friend you love and trust to look into your eyes and compliment you. Take in as many compliments as you can. If you reach a point where you are too uncomfortable to go on, ask your friend to stop. Repeat this process again a few days later, and see if you can take in more compliments this time.

Healing Process for Unborn Children

During the first trimester of pregnancy, you may wish to pray for your unborn child in the following way. Parents can also adapt this prayer for a child who is already born.

1. Light a candle and read Luke 1:39–56.

2. Close your eyes and breathe deeply. One or both parents place their hands on the mother's womb. Based on what you know of your child's develop-

ment at this stage, imagine how big your child is and how he looks.

3. Imagine Jesus, Mary, Joseph, and/or anyone else you trust placing their hands over yours. Breathe in their love for you and for your child. Breathe their love and yours out through your hands and into the child. Ask your child to tell you any hurts he may have experienced, including negative feelings you may have had about the pregnancy, thoughts of abortion, stress related to difficult circumstances in your own life, ingestion of toxic substances, and so on. Ask that the love you are breathing into your child touch those hurts. Listen for any ways your child may want to communicate forgiveness to you.

4. Share with your child your delight in him, and listen for how your child may want to thank you for giving him life. Thank God for the gift of this child.

First Trimester Game

Play hide-and-seek with your child, showing great delight each time you discover each other.

Chapter 5

Healing Twin Loss, Abortion, Miscarriage and Stillbirth

A deep hurt that often occurs during the first trimester (although it may happen at any time during the prenatal and perinatal period) is the loss of a child. In fact, many—perhaps most of us—have lost a brother or a sister. We say this because of the frequency of miscarriage, abortion, stillbirth and twin loss. In the United States approximately fifteen to twenty percent of pregnancies end in miscarriage, and Americans abort thirty-eight babies for every one hundred live births. Although the incidence of stillbirth has diminished greatly in recent years, at the time most of our readers were born there were two stillbirths for every one hundred live births. Embryologists estimate that thirty to eighty percent of us were conceived with a twin.

If we lost a twin in the womb, we may experience symptoms such as survivor guilt, irrational fear of death, or difficulty with intimate relationships (for example, always looking for the perfect companion, or sexual addiction in the form of a compulsive need to be near another body). If our mother had a miscarriage, abortion or a stillbirth and that loss was unresolved, we may have experienced our mother's womb as a burial ground, carrying the feeling of death. Moreover, if parents have not grieved a lost baby, they are unlikely to be emotionally available to fully bond with subsequent children. Just as in a broken marriage the previous spouse must be grieved before a healthy new marriage can be formed, so a lost child must be grieved before another child can be fully welcomed.

Praying for Lost Babies

Children are very sensitive to the loss of siblings, even when they have not been told about such losses. For example, Sue had six miscarriages before her daughter Julie was conceived. She had not grieved these miscarriages, nor told Julie about them. Julie was emotionally fragile and cried easily. She had six dolls about whom she seemed to feel anxious and responsible. Each had a name and each had to be accounted for at all times. After Sue experienced healing of the loss of her miscarried babies, Julie's attachment to the dolls diminished. They became toys she played with but did not worry about. Her mother now describes her as more lively and happy and less emotionally fragile.

We have led healing processes for thousands of women (and men) who, like Sue, have lost a child through miscarriage or abortion. We have always been deeply moved by how quickly the child forgives the parents and how critical this forgiveness is for healing of the parents' grief and guilt. Almost always the child desires an ongoing relationship with the parents and siblings, and often seems to become an intercessor whose protective presence the family continues to sense.

Healing Process (for Loss of One's Own Baby or for a Lost Sibling)

1. Light a candle. Close your eyes and breathe deeply. Recall a moment in your life when you knew how much God loves you. Breathe this love into yourself once again.

2. Get in touch with your feelings regarding the baby that died (love, sadness, longing, grief, guilt, anger, curiosity, etc.).

3. See Jesus, Mary, God the Mother, God the Father, or someone you love standing before you, holding your child or your sibling and offering him or her to you. Open your arms and receive the child. Say and do with the child all that your heart has always longed to do, and let the child do the same for you.

4. See what sex the child is and ask what name he or she wishes to be called. You may wish to baptize the

child. If so, make the sign of the cross on the child's forehead and say with Jesus, "I baptize you (name), in the name of the Father and of the Son and of the Holy Spirit." Imagine pouring water over the child's head, and feel the water cleansing and making all things new. Or you may wish to bless the child in some other way, consistent with your beliefs.

5. Talk over with the child how you can continue to give and receive love with each other. How do you want the child to pray for you and your family? How does the child want you to pray for him or her?

6. When you are ready, place the child in the arms of Jesus, Mary or God. See that instead of walking away from you, they walk *toward* you right into your heart. Feel their warm presence as they make their home in your heart. Breathe deeply, allowing that warmth to fill your whole body.

Healing Actions

1. Go to one of your favorite places, where you feel most able to give and receive love. In your spirit invite the lost child to accompany you. Share with him why this place means so much to you.

2. Ask yourself whom you would want as godparents for the lost child. Tell the child why you have chosen these people as godparents. Visit those people

and in your spirit bring the child with you. Invite the godparents to pray with you for the lost child and to bless him.

Game for Healing Loss of a Sibling

If you know that your child has lost one or more siblings, find a time when you feel especially connected to your child. Create a safe and warm environment, in which your child's favorite dolls or stuffed animals are nearby. Tell your child as much as you know about the loss. Ask your child if any of the dolls or stuffed animals want to say anything, or if she wants to say anything to or do anything with the dolls or stuffed animals. Follow the child's lead, and mirror back to the child any feelings she expresses. Talk over with the child what name to give the lost sibling. During the next days and weeks, offer the child additional opportunities to express any feelings about the loss with the help of the dolls or stuffed animals.

Chapter 6

Later Pregnancy

Throughout pregnancy, babies are spiritually and emotionally aware and responsive. In the later stages of pregnancy, they can reveal their awareness in more overt ways. For example, Dr. Franz Veldman teaches parents to make loving contact with their unborn child beginning in the second trimester. Dr. Veldman asks the parents to place their hands on the womb, and get in touch with all their love for their child. If they focus their love especially through the hands on the right side of the womb, the child will begin to move to that side and curl up with his or her neck under those hands. If they then focus their love through the hands on the left side of the womb, the child will move to that side and curl up under those hands. In this way, the parents can rock the child back and forth. If they do this at the same time each day and then miss their "visit" with the child one day, the child will begin to kick, as if in protest.

Babies may also use kicking to communicate what kind of music they like. For example, a study in a London hospital found that by four or five months in the womb, babies respond consistently to various types of music. They grow calm in response to Vivaldi and Mozart, whereas they become restless (indicated by kicking, etc.) in response to Beethoven, Brahms and hard rock music.

Babies communicate with their parents in many ways, some more obvious (such as kicking), and some in more mysterious ways. For example, in an experiment at Johns Hopkins University, 104 pregnant women were asked to predict the sex of their child based upon the way they were carrying the baby, a dream or just a feeling. Those who based their prediction on a feeling or dream were 71 percent correct, and 100 percent of those who cited a dream only were correct.

Fathers, too, can predict the sex of their child. Dr. Beatriz Manrique reports an experiment devised by a group of fathers attending her Hello Baby childbirth classes in Venezuela (mentioned in Chapter 1). The fathers wondered whether their baby would be a boy or a girl, but were too poor to arrange for sonograms. Each father told the baby in the mother's womb to kick once if it was a girl and twice if it was a boy. The next week in class they made a list of their answers. After the babies were born, Dr. Manrique checked the list. All ten fathers were right.

Hello Baby includes exercises for prenates developed by Dr. Rene Van de Carr at his Prenatal University program in Hayward, California. One of Dr. Van de Carr's exercises is the "Kick Game." Beginning in the fifth month of pregnancy and continuing through the third trimester, when the baby starts to make kicking motions, the parents can gently press where the baby kicked while saying, "Kick, kick." Eventually the baby may start kicking back. In some cases, once communication is established, each time the parents vary the number of presses the baby will respond with a similar number of kicks.

In another example of communication between parent and child, researchers Anthony DeCasper and Melanie Spence at the University of North Carolina did the following experiment:

> They asked pregnant mothers to read aloud *The Cat in the Hat*, a Dr. Seuss story, twice a day during the last six weeks of pregnancy. A few days after birth, the babies were given the opportunity to hear recordings of two stories, the familiar one and another Dr. Seuss story not heard before. Outfitted with earphones and a special nipple that let them change the story heard by sucking faster or slower, ten out of twelve newborns changed their speed of sucking to arrive at the familiar story.[1]

Babies in the womb respond not only to love, as communicated through a familiar story, but also to pain and stress. Because they are so sensitive and aware, they can be traumatized by the difficulties of their parents and also by many factors in the environment (including world events, as in Matt's example of World War II). In fact, when parents feel stress, prenates feel even more stress because they are so powerless and have so little defense.

Parents experience many stresses during the last months of pregnancy, such as changing or quitting jobs in order to be with the baby, taking on new jobs to make more money to support the baby or buy a larger home, and so forth. Mothers may be increasingly uncomfortable physically, and first-time parents especially may feel anxiety about childbirth. This can predispose the baby to anxiety later in life in any situation of transition (which symbolizes birth), such as college entrance exams, interviewing for a job or getting married.

Stressful life events during pregnancy need not cause lasting harm to the child if the mother feels loved and supported. In a review by researchers at Columbia University of over 144 studies, they concluded that intimate social support from a partner or family member substantially improves fetal growth. However, when this support is lacking, stress does affect babies. For example, Dr. D. H. Stott found a direct correlation between certain kinds of stresses in the mother during pregnancy and later physical and emotional problems in the child. The most problems resulted from prolonged stress in the parents' relationship. In his study of over thirteen hundred children and their families, Dr. Stott found that a woman in a tension-filled marriage runs a 237 percent greater risk of bearing a child with physical and emotional problems than a woman in a loving relationship.[2]

Medical interventions, such as sonograms, amniocentesis and other invasive procedures are also stressful for babies. For example, Dr. David Chamberlain writes:

Researchers have observed a strange response to withdrawal of amniotic fluid after amniocentesis. In this procedure, which has become increasingly common, a needle penetrates the womb to withdraw a sample of fluid to verify possible genetic defects. Prenates about sixteen weeks from conception were filmed after needle puncture by doctors in Denmark. Half of them showed a striking, somewhat ominous reaction: they didn't move for two minutes.

Half of them also lost the variations normally found in a series of heartbeats. This flat, unvarying heartbeat pattern is also seen in very sick babies or babies who have been hit by a dose of Valium or some other drug. Because none of the fetuses showed this pattern before amniocentesis, researchers conclude they were reacting to the procedure itself. What we see here is not indifference, but a sensitive, perhaps shocked reaction to what has just happened in the sanctuary where they live.[3]

Prenatal stress can affect babies so profoundly as to even alter their genes. According to biologist Dr. Bruce Lipton, genes do carry hereditary information, but they can be altered (at least partially) by environmental influences. When prenates grow in a loving and peaceful environment, the "peace and love" genetic triggers are activated, thus predisposing them to physical and emotional health. In a stressful environment, the "fight or flight" triggers are pulled, actually altering the DNA and predisposing babies to physical illness and emotional problems later in life, such as aggression and violence or fear and anxiety.

> Leading edge research in cell biology reveals that "environmental signals" are primarily responsible for selecting the genes expressed by an organism. This new perspective is in direct contrast with the established view that our fate is *controlled* by our genes. The new emphasis on nurture (environment) controlling nature (genes) focuses special attention on the importance of the maternal environment in fetal development.[4]

However, although the environment can alter genes to the extent of creating positive or negative predispositions, so far as is currently known the environment cannot actually override genetic defects. Thus, for example, a loving and peaceful environment cannot prevent a genetic disorder, such as Down's syndrome.

Although parents cannot eliminate all stress during pregnancy, they can minimize the harmful effects upon their baby. Psychotherapist Margaret Grant describes how she teaches her clients to do this:

> When a stressful situation occurs during a pregnancy, I teach the mother to visualize surrounding the baby with white light. I ask her to tell the baby that whatever is happening is not about the baby, that the baby is safe, and that mother will handle

the situation. I find this a very successful way of teaching babies boundaries before birth. I had a client who did intense emotional release work during her pregnancy. Before each session she would visualize her baby in white light, and tell him, "This is my time and my feelings. This is not about you." Then we would proceed with her session. Four weeks after the child's birth, she came for a session with him. She repeated what she had always told him and put him down beside her. He looked at me, looked at her, closed his eyes and went to sleep. Exactly fifty-five minutes later, after sleeping through his mother's loud release of anger and fear, he opened his eyes and looked at us calmly, as if to say, "Are you finished?"[5]

Because empathic presence is the greatest resource in resolving trauma, parents can help their babies immensely during the third trimester. If they recognize their baby as a conscious being who has thoughts and feelings about past experience, then the baby will not feel alone. If parents acknowledge any trauma that has occurred during the pregnancy (fights, ambivalence about the pregnancy, smoking, lack of awareness of their child as a conscious being, etc.) and ask the child's forgiveness, parent and child become partners in healing. Parents can also affirm the child's fears of birth and of life outside the womb, and pray with the child for healing.

Spirituality

Perhaps the greatest hurt for a baby in the womb is to be surrounded by parents and a culture that denigrate spirituality. If untraumatized, babies experience a profound sense of union with God of the sort that spiritual seekers may spend a lifetime trying to recover. This foundation of union forms a template and, as adults, such people are likely to remain open to the presence of God in all of life. However, if babies are traumatized and/or their spiritual sensitivity is not supported, this forms a template of defensiveness rather than openness. As adults, such people may expect life to be difficult and a struggle. Moreover, spirituality may become associated with pain. This can lead to an aversive reaction to God and all things spiritual (including one's own inner world), or to a rigid adherence to certain religious practices or beliefs in order to maintain control over the spiritual world. Such rigidity might take such forms as "Everything I need to know is in the Bible," "The Eucharist is everything," or "Only vegetarianism will save the world."

Conversely, a great gift to a child during this time is to be in an environment that fosters spirituality. Maybe this is why, in traditional Jewish culture, a pregnant woman would leave her husband and her other responsibilities and go to the home of a friend or relative who could provide care and seclusion. During her time away, she would pray, ponder the scriptures, and focus her thoughts on God in order to give her child a beautifully formed soul. Mary followed this custom when she visited her cousin Elizabeth for three months.

Healing Process for Oneself

1. Light a candle. Close your eyes and breathe deeply.

2. Imagine yourself in the womb. Ask yourself where your mother would have been most safe and loved as she waited for your birth. Perhaps you will think of the home of your grandparents, of another family member or of your parents' closest friends, perhaps a favorite family vacation place. If you cannot think of any safe place that was available to your mother, imagine a place to which you wish she could have gone, such as the home of Mary and Joseph, or the home of Mary's cousin, Elizabeth.

3. Now imagine your mother, perhaps accompanied by your father, going to this place. Hear the loving voices that surround your mother and feel the gentle ways in which people touch the outside of her womb, hoping to feel your tiny body. Breathe in the ways God is caring for your mother through her friends and family, as their love fills your mother and is transmitted to you across the placenta.

4. Place your hands over your navel. Ask yourself if there is any way in which you might have taken in wounding through the cord that once connected you and your mother. This might include toxic substances your mother ingested, knowingly or unknowingly. It might also include stress hormones

related to events in your parents' lives, such as difficulties in their marriage, financial problems, accidents, illness, deaths of loved ones, war or other forms of social upheaval, and the like. Perhaps your parents were simply anxious because you were their first child.

5. Use your hands to push away from your navel anything that came into you that you did not want.

6. Rest your hands on your navel once again, and once again breathe in the ways God is caring for your mother through her friends and family, as their love fills your mother and is transmitted to you across the placenta.

Healing Actions for Oneself

1. Find a safe, warm, clean place that smells good. Bring with you a cassette tape player and a favorite blanket. Wrap yourself in the blanket and listen to music by Mozart, Vivaldi or your favorite composer. Or you may wish to listen to "Transitions," a series of tapes of womb sounds combined with beautiful music. (Available from Transitions Music, P.O. Box 8532, Atlanta, GA 30306; 1-800-492-9885.)

2. At another time you may wish to ask a person you love and trust to help you with the above. Begin in

the same way and then ask that person to put their arms around the outside of the blanket and rock you back and forth, or stroke the blanket gently but firmly enough for you to feel his or her care, as you continue listening to the music.

Healing Process for Unborn Children

1. Close your eyes and breathe deeply, centering yourself in the love of God and breathing that love into the child you are expecting.

2. Ask yourself and your child where would be the safest and most loving place you could go where both of you (or all three of you, if the father is sharing in this prayer) would feel loved and cared for.

3. If possible, go to that place, even if for only a short visit. If you cannot go there physically at this time, go there in your imagination. While you are there, ask your child to help you recall or become aware of any times when toxic substances may have entered his or her body through the umbilical cord. Perhaps you experienced a stressful situation in which you felt overwhelmed by negative emotions. Perhaps you drank alcohol, smoked, took legal or illegal drugs or ate unhealthy foods. Whatever comes to you, talk over the situation with your

child. If it seems appropriate, ask your child's forgiveness.

4. Breathe in the healing love of God for yourself and for your child. Assure your child that you intend to do all you can to protect him or her and to care for yourself so that you will be able to transmit health to your child.

Chapter 7

Birth

I (Sheila) have indentations next to both of my eye sockets—the result of forceps that were used in my birth. The effects of birth trauma such as the use of forceps are far more than physical. For example, until recently I tended to feel frightened and agitated if anyone or anything moved abruptly in proximity to or toward my head. During games that used balls, I was likely to duck when the ball was coming toward me rather than catch it. I also tended to cringe or withdraw in the presence of people whom I perceived as intrusive or aggressive. Once I became aware that these behaviors could be related to the use of forceps at my birth, I began to imaginatively practice pushing the forceps away. My symptoms diminished and even my voice changed so that I no longer spoke with a tremor. The change in my voice is consistent with the work of Dr. Henry Truby. By analyzing the spectrographs of the voices of newborns he could determine which of a wide variety of prenatal and perinatal traumas they had experienced.[1]

As in the case of the forceps marks on Sheila's head, birth trauma is relatively easy to identify because it is imprinted upon the body. Almost anyone can learn to look at another person and determine which physical trauma they experienced at birth. For example, our friend Cris has a left shoulder that is lower than the right. Her left eye is lower as well, and her forehead is lower on the left side. Her spine forms a "C" curve to the left. Cris was probably lying on her left side in the womb and experienced a difficult birth that included a lot of compression. (The side on which a baby is lying is compressed most during birth.) Her body has carried the effects of her birth into adulthood.

When birth trauma is not treated in infancy, its effects are carried into adulthood. For example, the noted psychologist Nandor Fodor noticed that his clients had headaches, insomnia and attacks of various fears that correlated exactly with the time and day of their birth. When they made a conscious connection between their symptoms and traumatic aspects of their birth, Dr. Fodor's clients recovered.

To understand birth and its impact, it may help us to remember that in stressful situations human beings have two basic defenses: fight or flight. Babies at birth cannot do either—they cannot fight off the contractions and there is nowhere for them to flee. Nevertheless, birth does not have to be traumatic, and under ideal circumstances may be experienced as a joyful dance between mother and child. In our culture, birth often is traumatic because it is so far removed from the natural process it was meant to be. Most Western babies are born in hospitals, where the mother is commonly disempowered by the medicalization of the whole process. Women know how to give birth, each in her own way. In hospitals, however, there is usually only one way. Moreover, we often use obstetrical interventions that do save lives sometimes but often are not really necessary and can be very traumatic for the baby.

A common obstetrical intervention is the use of drugs, such as the Pitocin given to Laura (see Chapter 1). The American Academy of Pediatrics has issued a warning that no drugs have been proven safe for unborn babies, including obstetrical drugs. The danger of obstetrical drugs is compounded by the fact that they are prescribed on the basis of the mother's weight, which means a tiny baby receives an overdose.

When anesthesia is used during birth it can affect neurological development, cause brain damage from hypoxia (less oxygen than is medically deemed necessary) and increase the risk of substance abuse in later life. Karr-Morse and Wiley write that

> ...the routine administration of drugs during labor and delivery, once unquestioned, is being examined in relationship to later behavioral outcomes. Several studies indicate that the use of obstetrical anesthesia during delivery may cause subtle alterations in the formation of neurons, synapses, and neural transmitters that are undetectable at birth. One seven-year study of over three thousand babies showed long-lasting effects

of anesthesia on behavior and motor development. These babies were more likely to be slow to sit, stand, and walk. By age seven they lagged in language skills; their capacities for memory and judgment were also affected. Dr. Bertel Jacobson, a Swedish researcher, found a connection between adult addiction to opium and the use of opiates, barbiturates and nitrous oxide at birth.[2]

Other studies have found that anesthesia at birth can cause respiratory problems, such as emphysema, asthma and hyperventilation. People who have received such drugs may describe themselves as feeling "dazed" or "in a fog." And, strange as it may sound, we have witnessed healing processes during which we and others present in the room could smell anesthesia (especially ether) being released from the person's system—anesthesia that was used thirty, forty, fifty or more years ago when the person was born.

Another commonly used obstetrical intervention is cesarean section. Caesarean birth is sometimes necessary to save the life of the baby and/or the mother. Apart from life-threatening situations, it may seem desirable because it spares mother and baby the pain and struggle of passing through the birth canal and allows the birth to be scheduled at a "convenient" time. Actually, however, a caesarean robs the baby of the vital experience of his own power to push his way out and birth himself. Cesarean-born babies often have trouble completing things later in life because they weren't able to complete their birth.

Parents can educate themselves regarding these and other obstetrical procedures. They can refuse any interventions that are not truly necessary (including circumcision, which profoundly traumatizes most boys in our culture and which a growing number of medical professionals now recognize as harmful).

Parents Recapitulate Their Own Trauma

Most parents want to be emotionally present to their babies during pregnancy and at birth, but sometimes their own fears and unresolved traumas get in the way. For example, when Dennis and Matt's adopted sister, Mary Ellen, became pregnant, she was surprised by her negative feelings about being a mother. One day, she realized that these were not her own feelings. They were the feelings of her birth mother (who did not want her) that Mary Ellen had absorbed and was now reliving. This awareness allowed Mary Ellen to let go of her birth mother's feelings and experience her own deep joy in being a mother.

In general, women tend to give birth in the way that they themselves were born, recapitulating their own trauma. Moreover, other kinds of trauma are often evoked during birth. For example, as psychotherapist Dr. Michael Irving has observed, if the mother has been sexually abused, that memory is likely to be activated in her during delivery, because giving birth can be symbolic of sexual abuse in many ways. (For example, the mother's genital area is exposed to strangers, and the movement of the child through the birth

canal and resulting pain—which the mother cannot control—may be similar to the pain of sexual violation.) Not
only does the mother's traumatic experience of sexual abuse
permeate into the baby, but it can also interfere with the
actual process of birth.

In fact, Western culture's insistence that mothers give
birth lying on their backs (making labor and delivery more
difficult) rather than squatting, as in most non-Western cul-
tures, has its roots in sexual abuse. The French king Louis
XIV was sexually aroused by watching his mistresses give
birth to his children. He forced them to lie down because he
was not able to see well enough when they squatted.

What Parents Can Do

Despite all these possibilities for babies to be traumatized at birth, and many more that we have not mentioned,
parents can do a lot to prevent long-term negative effects.
Much of what follows also applies to adoptive parents, who
are also giving birth in their own way.

The first thing all parents can do is seek healing for
themselves prior to having a child, so their own birth and
other traumas will not permeate into their child. As they pre-
pare for their child's birth, they can request a *doula,* a
woman caregiver whose only task is to provide emotional
support for the parents during labor and delivery. Several
large studies by Dr. Marshall and Phyllis Klaus and Dr. John
Kennell have demonstrated the emotional and physical benefits of doulas. It seems that a woman is so emotionally open

and vulnerable as she gives birth that whatever happens at this time imprints deeply upon her and affects future behavior. If she is unconditionally affirmed by a doula who functions as a loving mother figure, this imprints upon her and can overcome years of negative messages from her own mother. It is as if she forms a new template for mothering. She will then instinctively and automatically pass on to her child the affirming love she has received, including during the birth process itself. The documented medical benefits of having a doula during birth include the reduction of first-time labor by an average of two hours, the reduction of cesarean sections by fifty percent, and the reduction of birth complications and need for pain medication.

The benefits of having a doula continue after birth. Women who have had a doula will show more maternal behaviors toward their newborns. As their children grow, these mothers are more likely to respond in unconditionally loving ways, passing on what they received from the doula. Fathers also report that having a doula helped them be more lovingly present to their wives and their new babies.[3] Adoptive parents can replicate the benefits of having a doula. For example, we (Dennis and Sheila) deliberately surrounded ourselves with unconditionally loving mothers and fathers as we waited for a baby.

When parents care for themselves in these ways, they will be able to care for their children. It is separation from loving caregivers that hurts babies most, whether literal physical separation after birth (such as putting babies in daycare at six weeks of age), or lack of emotional presence at any time during the perinatal period. Such separation vastly increases the chances of impaired bonding and attachment disorders, and the likelihood of aggression and violence in later life. According to Karr-Morse and Wiley, birth complications alone do not predict violence in later life. However, if a baby experiences birth complications and rejection or separation from his or her mother, the potential for criminal behavior in adulthood increases greatly.

Whether a stressful experience will cause lasting trauma depends upon whether or not we are enfolded in empathic, loving presence as we go through that experience. A baby who is born to parents who are out of touch with themselves, carrying unresolved birth trauma of their own, anesthetized, intimidated by medical personnel, or otherwise emotionally unavailable to that baby is likely to sustain trauma at birth. However, a baby whose parents are aware of what their child is experiencing and who empathically explain to their child what will happen during the birth process, is far less likely to sustain lasting damage, even if the birth is difficult. This is especially true if, as the child is being born and in the days and months that follow, they can compassionately verbalize the feelings they sense in their child.

Healing Process for Oneself

Repeat the Healing Process for Oneself on pages 18–20.

Healing Actions for Oneself

1. Ask a friend to accompany you to a playground that has a slide. Slide down, letting your friend wait for you at the bottom of the slide. Let your friend reach out and enthusiastically welcome you. Repeat this as often as you wish.

2. On your next birthday, plan the best possible celebration for yourself. Invite those who love you most to participate. Consciously take in their love for you.

Process for Healing a Baby's Birth

1. Light a candle and read Luke 2:1–18.

2. Close your eyes and breathe deeply. If you wish, sing *Silent Night* softly to your baby, as you breathe in the peace of that night.

3. In your imagination, place your baby in the crib at the stable in Bethlehem. See yourself and your baby's other parent touching and caressing your baby, with Mary and Joseph beside you.

4. Ask your baby what he or she most needs. Perhaps your baby needs protection from medication, or extra oxygen, or guidance in finding the way through the birth canal, or assurance that a cesarean delivery is not his or her fault, or to be shielded from the effects of unresolved trauma in your own life.

5. Whatever comes to you, breathe the love and protection of Jesus, Mary and Joseph into your child.

6. You may wish to end by once more singing *Silent Night* softly to your baby, breathing in the peace of that night.

Birth Games

1. This is a classic birth game, shared by many babies, that our John taught us (Dennis and Sheila) when he was two months old. If your child is still very small, hold her on your lap, lying on her back and with her feet against your stomach. Gently bend her legs and push her body forward toward your stomach. Encourage her to push away with her feet, saying things like, "You can push whenever you want to." When she pushes away, cheer for her. Be careful to hold her hands or cradle her head so that she won't fall off your lap.

2. This game may be helpful for trauma involving the umbilical cord. Notice if your child seems interested in cords, such as those for telephones or appliances. If so, give him one end of a piece of cord. Hold the other end, and let him pull on it. Resist briefly, but then let him pull the cord out of your hands.

3. Use your body to form a tunnel through which your child can crawl. With a very small child, you can

form the tunnel by standing or kneeling with your legs apart so the child can crawl through. Or you can kneel, then bend over and lean on your hands so a space is formed under your chest. Especially with an older child, you may wish to ask other family members to help form a taller, longer tunnel. Pairs of people can kneel or stand facing each other and join hands, so the child passes under their arms. As the child passes through the tunnel, cheer for the child and welcome him or her at the end.

Or take your child to parks or other places where there are slides or tunnels to crawl through. Welcome your child at the bottom of the slide or the end of the tunnel with cheers, a big hug and words like, "I'm so glad you're here!"

Chapter 8

Healing Early Wounding in Everyday Life

How important is it to figure out exactly what happened to us in the womb and at birth? On the one hand, it certainly can be valuable and very interesting to find this out, and a good therapist may be quite helpful in this regard. However, although professional help is sometimes necessary, we believe that the normal means of healing for most of us are loving relationships with other people, God and the natural world.

As the psychiatrist Graham Farrant often said, "If you want to know about someone's birth, ask them what is going on in their life right now." The way we would put this is to ask, "What do you most want now?" For example, if we are leaving on a trip and I (Sheila) ask Denny, "What do you most want?," he will say, "I want to leave early so I don't have to rush." Denny is telling me about his birth, when he was late and had to rush so that he wouldn't die. Matt will give a similar answer, "I want to leave early," but for a different reason. Matt will add, "in case we get stuck in road construction or traffic." Matt's reason reflects his birth, in which he got stuck in his mother's narrow pelvis and nearly died. If you watch me with John, now a very active seven-year-old, I will often say to him, "Honey, please don't move your toys so fast in my face." I am telling him about the forceps and my need to be able to protect my head. And John will often say to me, "Mama, be with me." He is telling me about being in the womb of his birth mother, who was not emotionally present to him.

Not only the behaviors we request of others, but even what we most want in our homes (colors, silence, music, water, furniture, etc.) can tell us about our earliest experience. For example, everyone in our family loves rocking chairs, and we have one in every room of our house, plus two rocking chairs (and a hammock) on our deck. Perhaps this is because neither Denny nor I were held enough as babies, and John spent his first eleven days after birth waiting to be gathered up in the arms of loving parents.

Empathy and Empowerment

Asking ourselves "What do I most want?" will usually reveal where in our lives we need empathy and empowerment, which are the two essential elements for healing early wounding. Empathy means loving presence, in which we compassionately try to enter into and understand the experience of another. Imagine, for example, that you have a friend who sits in the corner at meetings, stands behind her husband at parties, and generally makes herself as unnoticeable as possible, almost as if apologizing for taking up space. If you give her a compliment, she seems embarrassed and has difficulty receiving it. You can empathically carry in your heart for your friend the possibility—you are only guessing, but what matters is your loving intention—that she was rejected at the moment of discovery. You need never say anything about this to her. But whenever she comes to visit, you can take special care to welcome her. You can take an extra moment to look into her eyes and (but only if you mean it) say, "I am really glad you're here." The baby who still lives within her will sense your desire to understand; she will no longer feel so alone, and will be comforted.

Supposing you are the one who wants to hide. What can you do? You can become aware of the suffering of the baby within you, and you can ask a safe person to compassionately care for that baby with you.

In addition to empathy, the other essential element for healing is empowerment. Empowerment means experiencing your own power in present-day situations that resemble prenatal situations in which you were totally helpless. Thus, Dennis and Matt experience empowerment when they choose to leave early, and Sheila experiences empowerment when she protects her head from moving objects.

Children intuitively seek the empathy and empowerment they need to heal their early wounding, especially through play. They use their play to empower themselves and to show us what happened to them so that we can be empathically present to them. For example, one day when John was a toddler, he was playing with an empty suitcase. He climbed inside it, closed the lid over himself, then opened the lid and said to me (Sheila), "Mama, come inside with me." I understood that John wanted to be in a warm, safe, enclosed space with me...a womb. I said to John, "You want to be inside with me," and climbed into the suitcase with him.

Around the same time, John began another game involving the loose cotton Mexican dresses that I often wear. John would crawl in the bottom, hold on to me and ask to be lifted up inside the dress, saying, "I want to be an inside baby." Again, he was asking to be in a safe womb with me. Each time I lifted John up and carried him around with me inside my dress, I communicated to him, "I understand that you missed being inside the womb of a woman who could be fully present to you" (empathy), and "Now you can do something about it by climbing under my dress and showing me what you need" (empowerment).

We can trust children to show us what they need to heal their earliest wounds. Thus, children who were born by cesarean section, and therefore lost a sense of their own power to birth themselves, may look for opportunities to crawl through tunnels into the waiting arms of their parents. (At the end of John's last soccer game this year, the parents spontaneously formed a tunnel and invited all the children from both teams to run through it. We wondered how many of the parents realized the healing potential of what they had done.) Swings and slides, with their freedom of movement, can be deeply healing for children whose movement at birth was impaired due to forceps, anesthesia, or other medical issues. Children whose parents were not happy to discover they were pregnant often delight in playing hide-and-seek and experiencing their parents' delight in finding them. Children who ingested toxic substances through the umbilical cord, such as cigarette smoke, may feel a special exuberance in playing "firefighter," especially if they can find a big, long "hose." The hose may represent the umbilical cord, and this time the child has power over it. Similarly, children whose birth included cord complications, such as the cord wrapped around the neck, may seek out games involving cords and hoses, and parents can empower them by playing tug-of-war with the cord and letting the child win.

A Womb Surround

As we grew in understanding John's need for a safe womb, we (Dennis and Sheila) made him a "womb surround." A womb surround is a way of enclosing a person such that he or she re-experiences being in the womb. The shawls that third world women use to carry their babies on their bodies, or the American version known as a "baby sling," are a kind of womb surround. A group of people can form a womb surround by gathering around a child or an adult. Or, a womb surround can be made from fabric, cardboard, pillows, and so on.

After John outgrew his baby sling, we made him a womb surround from an old freezer box. We put the box on its side and cut a round hole for the entrance way. We put a soft pink quilt inside on the bottom, lined the walls with pink flannel, and draped pink silk from the ceiling. As a one- or two-year-old, at least once or twice a day John would dive into his womb surround and gesture for Sheila to join him there. John's womb surround has been empowering for him because he decides when he wants to be inside it, whom he wants to be with him, and what objects he wants there (nourishing food such as a jar of raisins, a flashlight to see with, etc.).

As an adopted child, John has a special need to experience himself in a safe womb with Sheila, his mother. However, all children need to experience their life after birth as being on a continuum with the safety of a healthy womb. We first understood this from Jean Liedloff's remarkable book, *The Continuum Concept*. The author spent two-and-a-half years living with a remote tribe of South American Indians. They were the happiest and most loving people she had ever met, and she attributed this to their child-rearing practices. For the first six to nine months of life, their children are in constant contact with the body of their mother or

another caring adult. They sleep with their parents and are breast-fed as often as they wish.

Thus, these children's lives after birth maintain the intimate closeness with their mother that they experienced in the womb. They are never put in cribs, baby holders, playpens, or other containers. Rather, the mother watches for signals of the child's gradually emerging desire for independence, and only then does she put him down to crawl or walk on his own.[1]

Because these children's early lives maintain continuity with the safety and intimacy of the womb, they are likely to carry within themselves an inner "womb surround" to which they can always return. Like John, we all need a womb surround that is ready and waiting for us.

Notes

Chapter 3

1. You may wonder what an adopted child is doing at his mother's breast. Actually, it is entirely possible for adoptive mothers to breast-feed as I (Sheila) did. I first learned about "adoptive nursing" from the popular parenting guide by William and Martha Sears, *The Baby Book: Everything You Need to Know About Your Baby—From Birth to Age Two* (New York: Little, Brown, 1993), pp. 183–184.

Chapter 4

1. For the effects of nicotine, alcohol and other drugs on the prenate, see chapter 3 of Robin Karr-Morse and Merideth S. Wiley, *Ghosts in the Nursery: Tracing the Roots of Violence* (New York: Atlantic Monthly Press, 1997). The quote is from pp. 60 and 62.

Chapter 6

1. Anthony DeCasper and Melanie Spence, "Prenatal Maternal Speech Influences Newborn's Perception of Speech Sounds," *Infant Behavior and Development* 9 (1986): 133–50.
2. D. H. Stott, "Follow-Up Study from Birth of the Effects of Pre-Natal Stresses," *Developmental Medicine and Child Neurology* 15 (1973): 770–87.
3. David Chamberlain, *The Mind of Your Newborn Baby* (Berkeley: North Atlantic Books, 1998), p. 55.

4. Bruce H. Lipton, "Nature, Nurture and the Power of Love," *Journal of Prenatal and Perinatal Psychology and Health* 13:1 (Fall 1998): 3–10. Quote is from p. 3.
5. Personal correspondence. Used with permission.

Chapter 7

1. Personal conversation between Henry Truby and David Chamberlain, reported in Chamberlain, *The Mind of Your Newborn Baby,* op. cit., pp. 68–69.
2. Karr-Morse and Wiley, op. cit., p. 76.
3. Marshall H. Klaus, John H. Kennell and Phyllis H. Klaus, *Mothering the Mother: How a Doula Can Help You Have a Shorter, Easier, Healthier Birth* (Reading, MA: Addison-Wesley, 1993).

Chapter 8

1. Jean Liedloff's ideas are gaining acceptance in North America, and have contributed to a growing movement known as "attachment parenting." See, for example, *The Baby Book,* by William and Martha Sears, a widely respected mainstream pediatrician and nurse.